for mom
whose love started it all

Before love

I remember the first time I saw you. Everything was dark. Your eyes. Your hair. The sound you made when you laughed. Your bangs were so long. You moved your head side to side, trying to outrun them. It never worked. I couldn't imagine the darkness that lived inside her. The shadows she left in the weakest parts of you. They weaved through your bones and tugged at your heart, the strings pulled too tight.

I remember the sound of slamming doors. Screams so loud the walls quivered. Insults hurled like plates at walls. He left us for good that time. Bags ready at the front door. A single wave from a window too tinted to see through it. My heart broke that day. Five years old and three feet tall, you left a hole in my chest that would last a lifetime. He didn't look back. Not for her. Not for us. Not for anything.

you first learned
to love
from your mother
a twisted woman
who found flaw
in your design
and favour
in your pockets
her love
was reserved
for her throat
her nose
and her veins
you were nothing
but a reminder
of all the ways
she tried to disappear

I first learned
to love
from my father
a reckless man
who found access
in my adoration
and opportunity
in my innocence
his love
was reserved
for his ego
his self
and his desires
I was nothing
but a reminder
of all the reasons
he tried to leave

it's no wonder
we never made it
till the end
how can
two people
who learned love
was something
to escape
ever choose
to stay?
-kc

First love

I couldn't help but wonder what your hands would feel like. The calluses against my skin from the guitar you always carried. I never thought of whispers. Or stares. Sidestepping if I got too close. I didn't think about the category I'd fall into by falling for you. I only thought of that shy smile. The eyes that reminded me of melted chocolate. I was so intrigued by you. What did it mean? This desire to learn every little thing about another girl. Desire became necessity. If I did not learn you, know you, love you, I was certain I would die without you. It was all consuming and all confusing. And I think that saved me as much as it ruined me. I did not, would not, could not, think of anything but you. That left no room for worrying about what people thought of me. Of you. Of us. That left no room for anything at all.

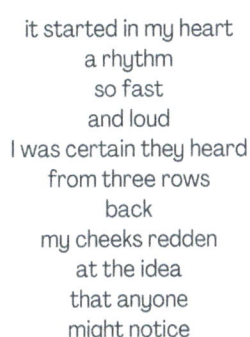

it started in my heart
a rhythm
so fast
and loud
I was certain they heard
from three rows
back
my cheeks redden
at the idea
that anyone
might notice

I was confused
when she sat down
third row
from the front
it wasn't her hair
the swoop bang
or her bracelets
black
not the band tee
beneath the uniform
she wasn't allowed
to wear

it was that she
was a she
and not he
like all the times
before
my first love
was a she
before I knew
I could love
a she
just like me
-kc

During love

I wish it wasn't always the same. Every relationship. Every girl. It could be three months in. Seven. Fourteen. It came in silence. A nudge so subtle, I wasn't sure it was real. Or maybe that's what I told myself. So I'd stay. Let the days, or weeks, or months, pass. The false sense of conviction I built would crumble, doubt swift in its wake. Slowly, I let the walls close in until the only choice left was to leave. I asked you when I'd know if I found the one, and you told me I just would. That was it. The question of if would die, and only certainty would remain. But as time went on, and lovers became exes, I found a flaw in your theory. How can I recognize something if I was never shown what to look for? Is it possible to rely on a feeling, when I was shown that love was only found in its leaving?

they tell me I'll know
when I feel it
so I wait
and wait
and wait
I know nothing

when I'm unsure
if I know
I leave
again
and again
and again
I have nothing

    I want to know
what they mean
so I search
and search
and search
I find nothing

        did they know
when they told me
love
is a feeling
I'll know
that I was shown
by a man
whose love
was found
in his leaving

            turns out
in the end
they know nothing
-kc

In love

Do you remember when we moved you into that apartment? It was your first one without me that wasn't your parents. We carried boxes of your belongings to a room that wasn't ours. Placed things in a bathroom that used to crowd our own. I remember thinking *if I fold these sheets just right, if I plump this pillow just so, if I move this table as such, it will feel like home*. I wanted it to feel like home, you know?
It didn't.
You've moved since. So have I. More than once. Place after place I fold the sheets just right, plump the pillow just so, and move the table as such. To make it feel like home.
It doesn't.
Did you know I stopped at the end of the lot? My rearview mirror no longer held you. Barefoot in sweats, framed by the light in someone's else's doorway. I almost turned around, afraid to move on without you.
I couldn't.
I guess what I'm wondering is, have you found it yet? The place that feels like home? Because I've been thinking lately. Maybe the key to home is the people in it. Maybe for ours to be found we have to be together in it.

I wanted to write
with all the wisdom
and all the wonder
of a woman
finally
truly
in love
but all I found
inside me
was the truth
that I have no idea
what in love
really is
yet
this story
like many others
is still
in the process
of being written
and when it's finished
I can tell you
my in love
will feel a lot like
returning home
to myself
-kc

After love

Your name slipped from my lips before my brain could tell it not to. We hadn't seen each other in over a year. Hadn't spoken in just as long. I cut you off, cold turkey. The quick-fix method for getting clean. Fitting, isn't it? You always were my drug of choice. It was my birthday. The universe had a sense of humour. Want a birthday gift? How about the one thing you always wished for but never got?

I thought I wouldn't care. I did. Seeing you felt like chewing on lightning and choking on fireworks. Your eyes drank me in with a thirst that left the room bare. She stood next to you, and my heart hurt for the beauty we'd never become together. Helpless at the way your eyes dimmed with shadows where our light went out. Breathless, I walked away from you. Our someday sealed in the concrete footprints I left behind.

the more I try
to let her go
the more ways
I find her
coming back
like waves
in a storm
at dawn
her eyes pull me in
a dance
as blue
swirls
gray
with ink
along the edge

I falter
daylight wanders in
and I notice
her eyes are the sea
sometimes blue
sometimes gray
always distant
never calm
-kc

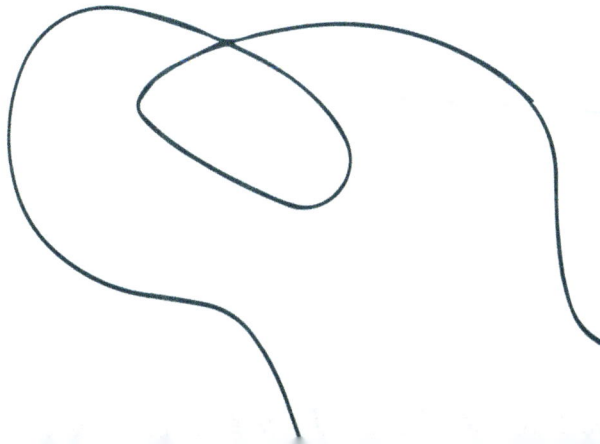

Forbidden love

I always picture the truck you drove. Gold. A little dirty. It wasn't yours. The dash covered in dust. You wore a white t-shirt. Taut on your chest. Wet under your arms. It was hot that summer. Always. So. Hot. I think I made you nervous. Was that why you were always so sticky? Or was it summer?

It clung to our skin in the evenings, well after the sun left us dark. You held me that afternoon, your fingers tracing invisible lines on my arm. We were the closest we'd been. But not too close. Careful. I told myself it was because of summer.

Wasn't it?

In my bed that sleepy, sweaty, sunny afternoon, it was me and you. In that moment, the world became so small. For a second, I almost believed there wouldn't be enough space for her in it.

Almost.

I thought at one point
we'd be friends again
we were friends once
I think
I liked the connection
washed in heat
when our skin kissed
that first night
once the dust settled
I used to think
yeah
we can get back there

but when summer came
she told me
my soul knows you
even more
that our connection
is so intense
because we have lived it
many lives
before

we used to be in love
she tells me
the way two
inexplicably
become one
and the knot
that curls
around the heart
in my chest
is not the pain
of forgetting
but the ache
of remembering
-kc

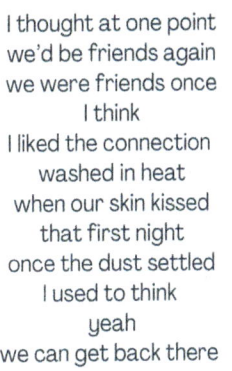

Secondhand love

The room was filthy and dark. I spotted you from across the bar. Beer stuck to my heels when I moved closer. You wore a snapback, a sleeve of tattoos running up your arm. She begged me to leave. The bar was dead. Too dead for a Friday. I relented. I looked at you, hoping you'd catch my eye.
You didn't.
We ended the night at a diner full of drunk students with a table of boys we'd never met. The one next to me shook someone's hand. It was yours. You were friends with them. This table of boys we didn't know before tonight. No sooner had we said hello and you disappeared. I lost you, again.
That would become our thing, though I didn't know it then. Me searching, you staying lost. The girl with the blond hair and the tattoos on her arm.
Heading for the exit someone called out for me. It was you.
What's your tattoo say?
I smiled, walked closer.
You and I?
That was only the beginning.

I held the cigarette between my teeth
loose
careful not to crush the paper
I took a long drag
slow
careful not to burn the edge
you held my heart in your hands
loose
careful not to feel too much
you took a long pause
slow
careful not to leave too loud
I let go while it kept burning
stomped
until it went out
you let go while I was still burning
stomped
until I went out

-kc

Foreign love

I worry, on the nights I'm too tired to believe otherwise, that I will never have my great love. The one all the books are written about, and the songs, and the movies.

When I was young, I didn't dream of a house full of kids, or a wedding suffocated in tulle. I dreamed about love. Big, outrageous, magical, write-a-novel-about-it love. I wanted to build a life with someone who made me feel the way I imagine home is supposed to.

Safe. Supported. Held. Free. Loved.

But the more lovers I had, the more hearts I collected, the further away it felt. I'm afraid to trust myself in making a choice.

So I don't make one. I leave.

How can I declare forever on a feeling I've never had?

today
I'm ready to dive in
head first
tomorrow
I might run so far
you disappear
I never know
what is stronger
the pull
to love you
or the demand
to leave
-kc

Selfish love

I thought you could love me enough for the both of us. If anything could save me, it would be the gentleness of your heart, and the space it made for me. Or your hands, and the delicacy as they traced the edges I'm made of.
I wanted to protect you. Safeguard your softness against the darkness I carried.
When you left for work in the mornings, I'd pretend to be asleep. Careful not to show you the clouds I wake with.
I'd lie there all day, unshowered, unmoving, undone.
But every night, when you came home from work, the bed was made, my teeth were brushed, dinner was ready.
The only energy I had in a day was spent convincing you I was someone I wasn't.
I wanted to be her, you know. The girl you came home to.
No one wanted her more than I did.
Not even you.

she told me once
of the great indecision
how she sent you away
and wished for you back
on
and off
and on again
and it broke my heart
to think
of all the love
we leave behind
because we believe
we aren't worthy

I thought of us
how I brought you back
and wished you gone
on
and off
and on again
and it broke my heart
to think
of all the love
we resurrect
because we're scared
of letting go

I wonder
is there another way
to love
and be loved
will we ever learn
the difference
between holding on
and letting go?
-kc

Imaginary love

The air was summer morning warm, a breeze tickling loose strands of sweaty hair across my cheek. We sat facing the street, two cups of tea between us, when a car drove by. Her car. You'd been at lunch with your mom. We made eye contact and I could feel it. Like an elastic band snapping between us. The glance wasn't more than a second and I was reaching for my phone, already knowing what I'd find.

Your name appeared, taking up too much space. I told myself I didn't care in the same breath I wished I didn't. As your words filled my screen, fire flooded my veins. You spoke of how hard it was to see me look so good.

The pain in your heart my presence caused. For a moment, it felt real again. We felt real again. Like sharpened knives stuck in my chest, each word twisted deeper than the last.

Concern filled my friend as she asked what was wrong.
Reality resumed.
I said it was nothing.
Because it's true. We are not real.
We are, and have always been, nothing.

inside I'm screaming
what was the point?
but I'll never ask you
the conversations we had
polite chatter and weekend maybes
turned daily musings and constant connection
the secrets we shared when the night came
and the feelings we confessed before the sun rose
the time you found me in a crowd of people
and told me how you always would
suddenly I became your person for all the things
and we began to plan our someday
there were trees and water and dogs in the yard
in the middle of nowhere, finally together
you had my heart before you even held my hand
and as I packed my bags to meet you
you changed passengers
while I reached as far as I could
to pull my heart outside my chest
and give it to you
you left it on my doorstep and drove off
in a car that belonged to someone else
the hardest part
wasn't the change in plans
or the change in person
the hardest part
was finally understanding
my falling in love
was just your Tuesday afternoon
-kc

Single love

I want to be mad at the ones whose love failed me. But if I was, I'd have to be mad at myself. Those who left were given no other choice. Their exits the only response to a nightmare I created. I can't remember who I wrote this about. Night after night I come back to this page, no closer to the answer. Far from the truth. Maybe it's because there was never just one person. There was no one time.

This revelation arrived at every end I met. Asserted my independence like they needed a reminder. Shoved it down their throats and watched while they choked on it. Taking up all the space until one of us vanished. It left me alone to prove that I could. It left them heartbroken that I felt like I should.

I haven't figured it out yet, but I'm in the season of knowing I can handle things alone, and letting someone in anyway.

Sometimes breakfast is better with two.

I thought I needed all these great things
to have a great love
and I thought I needed all these great things
to be happy
but I realized I can be great things
on my own
and I can be happy
on my own
what I can't be
is loved by you
on my own
-kc

Sick love

I thought it was love I felt. It had to be. What else could describe the magnetic pull? The desire for you always outweighing the consequences of it. The lines often blurred. I did things I shouldn't. Hurt people I loved.
All for what, exactly?
That's the part I have trouble remembering. I chased you like a high I couldn't get enough of and you kept me nearby in case you decided you wanted me. You used me and I let you because I told myself I loved you.
I didn't.
I loved the idea of the person I thought you were. I loved the picture in my head of the couple we could be. It took everything in me to let you go.
One relapse to teach me who you really are.
Staying with you was me loving you.
Cutting you off was me loving myself.

our love was my addiction
with you as my enabler
only one sip, you said
just a line, you promised
I'm two years clean
can you believe that?
two years sober
since the night on my floor
with the empty bottles and broken mirrors
white blurs and liquid burns

we pretended it was love
side by side in naked chaos
your hand around my neck
when you held me as your one
your eyes filled with forever
until I let you go
and my 12 steps finally told me
addicts can't be lovers
-kc

Explosive love

When you call me I don't answer. I don't see the point. I told you as much. You laugh like I'm kidding. You want to be friends.
Is that necessary? Do exes need to be friends?
Our ending wasn't amicable. It wasn't even courteous. It was brutal, painful, and drawn out. I broke your heart. You broke civility. Honestly, I can't say I blame you. You have every right to be upset. To hate me. But you don't.
You want to be friends.
I consider it.
Years have passed, we've changed. Friends could work, I think.
And then I saw you.
The only way to describe it would be heat underneath every single inch of my skin, trying to get out. Your presence left no air for me, standing outside in the drive. You made a few jokes, trying to ease the tension. I kept my distance, afraid of what could happen.
Would it start a fire, if I touched you?
Would we put it out, if it did?

what I feel
is inconvenient
returning at a time
too late
a fire so sudden
my insides
turn
to ash
yet I stand here
feet planted
as your eyes dance
the dare in them
a cause for overwhelm
the curve of your smile
and how it lifts your cheek
weakens me
as our fingers brush
I swear
for a second
I could.
not.
breathe.
dodging flames
from a fire
long ago started
running
with not an end
in sight
-kc

Splintered love

I know you think I broke up with you because I was over you. Somewhere inside you tell yourself I stopped loving you. That the first girl I dated afterwards meant something. You probably think it was easy. That I could turn it off like a key in the lock.
You'd be wrong.
Painfully, ridiculously, cartoonishly wrong. Leaving you wasn't a switch between on and off. It was a crack in the very centre of my heart that never healed. It was endless nights for years asking myself what I was thinking. It was doubt so crippling my muscles ached. It was late night ice cream binges and too many journal entries and questions left unanswered and burning regret that split me in two.
Leaving you was a lot of things.
I can promise you, easy was never one of them.

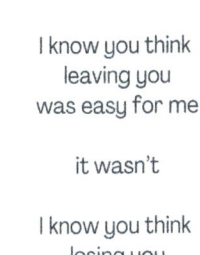

I know you think
leaving you
was easy for me

it wasn't

I know you think
losing you
was better for me

it wasn't

I know you think
loving you
is over for me

it isn't

-kc

Fractured love

I could write a list of all the ways I let you down, but it would be short.
Just one. I left. I did it.
Did the thing I shouldn't do. The thing I swore I'd never do. I haven't been able to write about it. There was something about bringing it from my heart, to my head, to the screen, that felt impossible. Like an answer that was too late. A sorry left unsaid.
Admitting I left you meant revealing the other half of the truth. I chose. It wasn't a loss that happened to me, but one that I made. And I couldn't write about it.
Because writing's my mirror.
It sees all and says all.
And I wasn't ready to hear it.
Does that make me a coward? Maybe. Would I leave again, if I could go back? Definitely.
Because the choice was never to stay or go. It was only to survive.
One more day.
Moment by moment until I led myself out of a darkness threatening to ruin us both.

I knew before I drove away
you would never understand
I chose to live with that
standing barefoot in the darkened doorway
heartbreak joined the shadows
etched in the features I'd come to memorize
I watched you watch me walk away
from you
from home
from us
your stance was a test
we both knew I'd fail
and I did
you wanted me to choose you
and home
and us
like it was that simple
I wanted to ask you
did you ever wonder
if I wanted that too?
because it was never a choice
between what I wanted
and what I didn't
it was a choice between
trying to swim
or letting you drown
and I would rather watch you
breathe without me
than live knowing
you sank within me
-kc

Messy love

When I least expect it, grief walks in.
He leaves his boots on. Mud streaks the floors. Dirties the carpets. I put a hand on my chest to protect what's coming, like I can stop it.
I can't.
He grabs a hold of me so tight the breath gets stuck in my mouth. He wants me to face him. To look him in the eye and admit he's there. He got me. I'm his.
I thought I was done.
I couldn't take another bruise that didn't colour. Another break that didn't show. People don't understand what they can't see. They couldn't grasp what grief made of me. It clung to every part like saran wrap on my organs then demanded I live.
I couldn't.
I must.
It's always something simple that reminds me of you. Unexpected. Like the voice of someone who sounds like you used to. Homemade bread in a kitchen you never cooked in. Crumpled tissues in a jacket I forgot about. I don't see it coming, and then there you are, vivid in my mind but never in the street. What comes next is what hurts. It's where he wins. When the pieces of you vanish and I'm reminded you're already gone.
That the memories I have of you are finite.
I'll never make any more.
He got me. I'm his.

it was anger
first
not loud
like holes
in the wall
or glass
in shards
by the bed

quiet
like smoke
in your lungs
or fire
in flames
by the throat

then came grief
second
not quiet
like tears
in the sleeve
or liquor
in veins
by the couch

loud
like sirens
in your mind
or screams
in pain
by the door
-kc

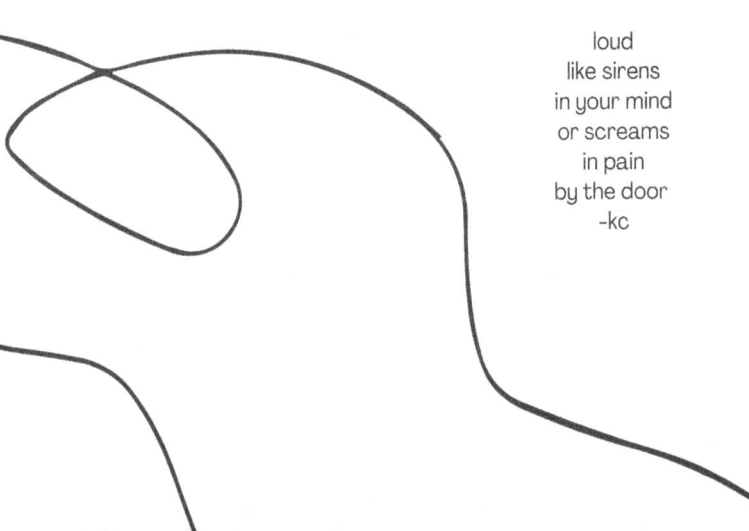

Forever love

When I let you go, I told myself it was just for now. In my head, this was only ever temporary. It was how I was able to leave. How I packed my car, drove east, and put miles between us.

I held onto that for years. A balm over my heart for the guilt I felt breaking yours. It made sense at the time, in all my grief and sorrow and ruin.

Can you see that now?

The impossible choice of hurting you by leaving so I wouldn't destroy you by staying. Back then, I was so close to choosing you. Car in reverse, foot on the gas close. I would've chosen you over anything, or anyone. But I made a promise when I was young, after I gave all of me to someone who decided they didn't want me anyway. I promised myself I would always choose me first.

No matter what.

I would never again surrender all my love to someone else, if it meant leaving nothing for myself. There was only one choice back then.

Me, or you.

I honoured my promise.

I see now, what I couldn't then. There was a third choice, nestled beneath the darkest thoughts.

Us. Me with you.

I'm sorry I couldn't see it until now.

I have written so many poems
about other loves
but not once
have I written
about you
not once
have I written
about ours
and I never thought
to question why
until today
when the first one
touched the page
and I realized
I only write these poems
about the ones I love
when the love
becomes past tense
and my heart broke
a second time
to feel the ending
to a love I thought
would never grace these pages
a story I thought
would never end
-kc

Interrupted love

Whenever I hear the song Can't Shake You I'm back in time. Sitting on the roof of your shed in the crisp, spring air. It's nighttime, and your friends are scattered in and out of the house, distracted. I've never been here before, but I'm pretty sure I never want to leave. Some of them are swimming in water much too cold, with only the moon to light their way. It's so dark out, all I can see is the gold in your hair and the whites of your eyes. We had whole conversations with only that gold and white. Until I made you laugh.
Then it was your smile.
I remember thinking to myself, there is nothing else in this world that matters to me more than seeing that smile. I want to be the reason it shows up, every day, forever. I fell in love with you in an instant. That's what I remember most.
One second, I'm laughing with you.
The next, I'm falling for you.
I belonged to you, even though you never asked me to. I wasn't ready for it. We might be together today, sitting on rooftops, laughing in the moonlight, if I was. A season of love, exchanged for a lifetime.
If I close my eyes, I can almost see it.

you were my summer
with your long
sunshine
hair
and bright
sea glass
eyes
sharing rooftop laughs
at dawn
and favourite books
in bed
your smile both familiar
and new
I thought I could love you
in a way
that would last
forever
but like summer
you were always leaving
much
too
soon
-kc

Broken love

By the time we met, I was nothing more than a shell of my former self. I sat on your couch, eyes bloodshot. Coloured wrong by too many nights of drinking in excess. Basic hygiene had become difficult. I knew when I woke up that morning, on the floor of a bedroom I didn't recognize, I needed help. A heaviness held me before I said a word. She pushed a box of tissues forward on the coffee table between us.
An offering.
So I told her. For 50 minutes, I talked about you. The pain you caused me. The love I had for you anyway. Split in two by the desire to leave and the need to stay. I wasn't sure why I went to see her, not entirely.
What was she going to do?
She smiled kindly, the wrinkles around her eyes a mark of all the wisdom meant to find me. She spoke, the only words I needed.
Look in the mirror behind you. You must leave. Leave for her. Leave because you have to. Because staying is killing you. And if you do not leave now, I can guarantee you, it will be too late. If you don't go now, there will be nothing left of you to leave with.
The bell rang. Our time was up.
The session ended. I thanked her, took the box of tissues, and left. The room. The office. The relationship.
You.
The answer to my question earlier, of what she could do, finally answered. She gave me permission.

it was anger I met first
her greeting subtle
and unmistakable
like a closed door
whose other side
licked flames

sadness came second
her arrival obvious
and heavy
like an ocean wave
whose first break
carried sand

but it was love
both subtle
and obvious
that still remained
amongst the ashes
of your fire
and the whispers
in the grain
-kc

Restricted love

It didn't look like winter. At least, not the ones I'm used to. There was no snow on the ground, gathered in banks off the road. No white dusting on trees, masking lonely branches. The air was crisp and cool, not yet cold. We drove with the heat on low, already shedding hats and jackets. When I told you I was going alone, you offered to come. I should have said no. Protested with a carefully crafted excuse.
I said yes.
It was a test, though I couldn't tell if you knew.
You did.
Standing at the door I waited for the inevitable *I'm sorry*, when *I'm here* came instead.
When we arrived, you pulled a blanket from the trunk and placed it on the concrete steps. Together, we took a seat, our thighs touching. Body heat, you told me. We sat like that until we couldn't feel our fingers; the chill only slightly greater than my sorrow. On the ride home, I was unusually silent. Tears fell from my eyes too quickly to catch them. I never was one for vulnerable moments in the company of others, but with you, I managed. My head faced the window, fingers tapping out an anxious beat.
Is this okay? you asked, reaching for my hand.
I remember thinking it was the most okay I'd felt in a really long time.

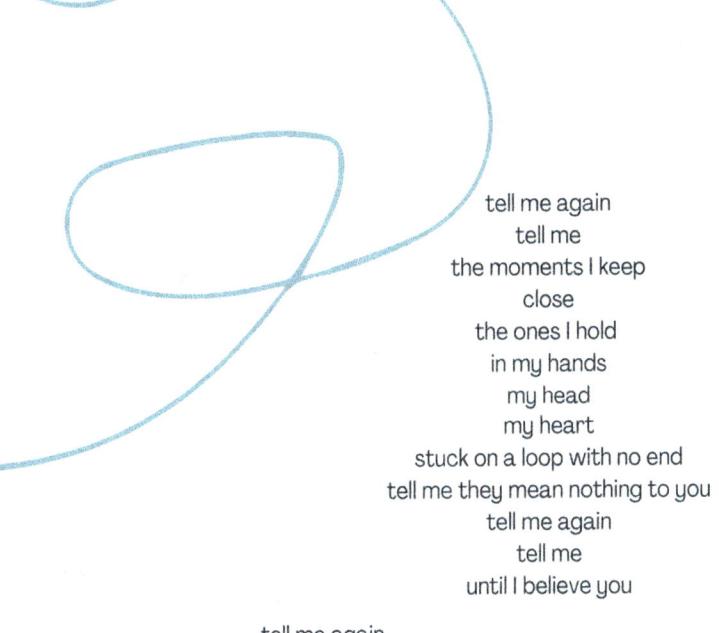

tell me again
tell me
the moments I keep
close
the ones I hold
in my hands
my head
my heart
stuck on a loop with no end
tell me they mean nothing to you
tell me again
tell me
until I believe you

tell me again
tell me
the aches I wear
inside
the ones I feel
in my head
my lungs
my chest
caught between body and breath
tell me they don't happen to you
tell me again
tell me
until I believe you
-kc

Rare love

We sat in silence across the room in separate chairs. The space between us crowded with what we couldn't say. I tell you to scoot over. Your chair was big enough for two, I promised.
And it was.
Barely.
What were you showing me? I can't seem to remember. The chair shifted slightly beneath the weight of us, straining to hold us both. From ankles to shoulders, our bodies touched. It felt like an electrical current connecting our veins. Buzzing under my skin, competing with the sound of my racing heart. I felt you relax, a sense of peace settled between us.
Finality.
Like when you put the last piece of a puzzle together, and the whole picture is revealed. It was clear to me then. Clearer when you stood to leave. I'm tethered to you. Even on the days I don't want to be. Even when I can't be.
I am.
I've tried to break it. Move around it. Love over it. Change it. But I can't. It's not up to me. It was never up to me. Who we are to each other goes beyond what I can control.
All I can do is wait for what is certain.

I'm terrified
you are the only person
in existence
who is honestly
truly
deeply
meant for me
I'm terrified
because
you are not mine
and I not yours
yet
we have this belonging
this intensity
that binds us
whether we are moments
or months
or years
apart
I'm terrified
I will never love another
if my heart
only beats
for you
-kc

Departed love

It came together in a matter of days. There wasn't time for debating, or contemplating, or changing our minds. We agreed I'd be the one to speak, though it wasn't really a service. Mom opted for something less sorrowful. There would be speeches, a chance for those who loved her to share their stories. I volunteered. It made sense, like it always has, for it to be me. To shelter my sisters from as much as I could. When it was time, I stepped up to the microphone, and looked around at everyone we loved, everyone who loved you.

I took one look at the crowd, with all my quiet strength, and sobbed.

Great, painful, hideous sobs. The kind that couldn't be contained in my body, coming out instead in strangled sounds that echoed off the walls. It was so unexpected a nervous hush fell over the crowd.

I could do this. For you, I would. I must.

And I did.

I told stories that made people smile, and laugh, and cry. I talked of your strength, your unfailing kindness towards others, and the depth of your love that always felt endless. I let your presence fill the room through my words and watched as the others held onto it. Held onto you. And when I was done I said goodbye, here, in this room.

Knowing I'd keep you forever, here, in my heart.

I remember
being covered
in grief
the damage so dense
it stained
my clothes
and turned
my ruby lips
white
the sounds I made
went silent
the screams
so loud
you felt them
leave
-kc

Self love

You tell me I'm beautiful, or pretty, or sexy, and I thank you. I don't question it, or deny it, like I used to. Progress, right?

It doesn't matter.

The words you say to me, whispered in bed between goodnight kisses and floating in doorways of crowded rooms, simply disappear. They vanish, their truth swept away in a question I can't answer.

Is it me?

Is it that I don't find myself beautiful, or pretty, or sexy? That doesn't seem right. It's not that you don't mean it, and it's not that I don't believe you mean it. It's almost like, I know you mean it and I think you're incorrect to feel that way.

It feels fake.

Duplicitous.

Like I'm trying to be beautiful, or pretty, or sexy, in certain moments. And when I'm doing that, I know you're going to think it too. I've set it up so you will. And it makes the whole thing feel planned. So when you compliment me, it's nothing more than a trap I've laid for you. Why do I do that? Why do I set myself up to disprove you? It feels like strangers in a room full of masks, and I'm just another person playing my part. What is my mask? Do I know who I am without it? Am I willing to find out?

I do not look
inside myself
often
I fear what I might find
buried deep
in my soul
if I had a mirror
to show me
what lies within
I fear the goodness
that I wish
is merely
the darkness
that I am
-kc

Unknown love

It's not that I didn't want to know. Or didn't try to know. Because I did. I was in love with love by the time I could read. Huddled in my closet next to stacks of books, I'd read about all the girls who met all the boys and fell in love.
There was fast love and big heartbreak and a grand romantic gesture to bring it all together. I told myself it's what I wanted, even if some of the pieces didn't quite fit. Flipping through pages gave me happy endings and characters who always found their way back to each other.
I'd look at my surroundings and compare.
Around me there was absence and threats and broken homes.
Was that love outside of novels?
It wasn't until I was older, experiencing my own fast love and big heartbreak, that I realized I didn't know. Books are tales born from imagination, not limited by the construct of reality.
My idea of love grew from those tales, and when I met the real thing, I fell promptly, naively, on my face.

it was still dark out
the moon
not yet
the sun
you set your eyes on me
one arm
around my waist
three words
on your lips
without thought
easy
as
breathing
you smile yourself to sleep
a siren in the silence
I lay beside you
rigid with certainty
I don't know what love is
-kc

Shadow love

You didn't have to come. My plane landed late at night, you like to sleep early. You insisted. Pulled the car up and got out to meet me.

I dropped everything to hug you. It lasted two seconds too long. Did you count too? I was beaming from my travels. A week with my best friends in the mountains was good for me. Too good. I was thinking of moving. Across the country, in fact. We started driving, the silence frostier than the air outside.

It's nothing, you promised.

But it wasn't nothing, was it? It was never nothing. Slowly, the pieces of us, no more than duct tape covered hearts, crumbled. One by one, we came apart, the cracks so big this time I knew we couldn't fix it.

You were crying. I couldn't see beyond the red of my anger. It shouldn't matter, you tell me. It shouldn't matter what you want if all I want is friendship, right?

Wrong.

You wanted me to go first. To tell you it was real.

I refused.

I won't reveal my hand when you keep leaving the game. It's your turn. To stay. To tell me it's real.

You didn't.

I don't let myself think about it often. But when I do, I wonder.

Who would we be to each other, if you had?

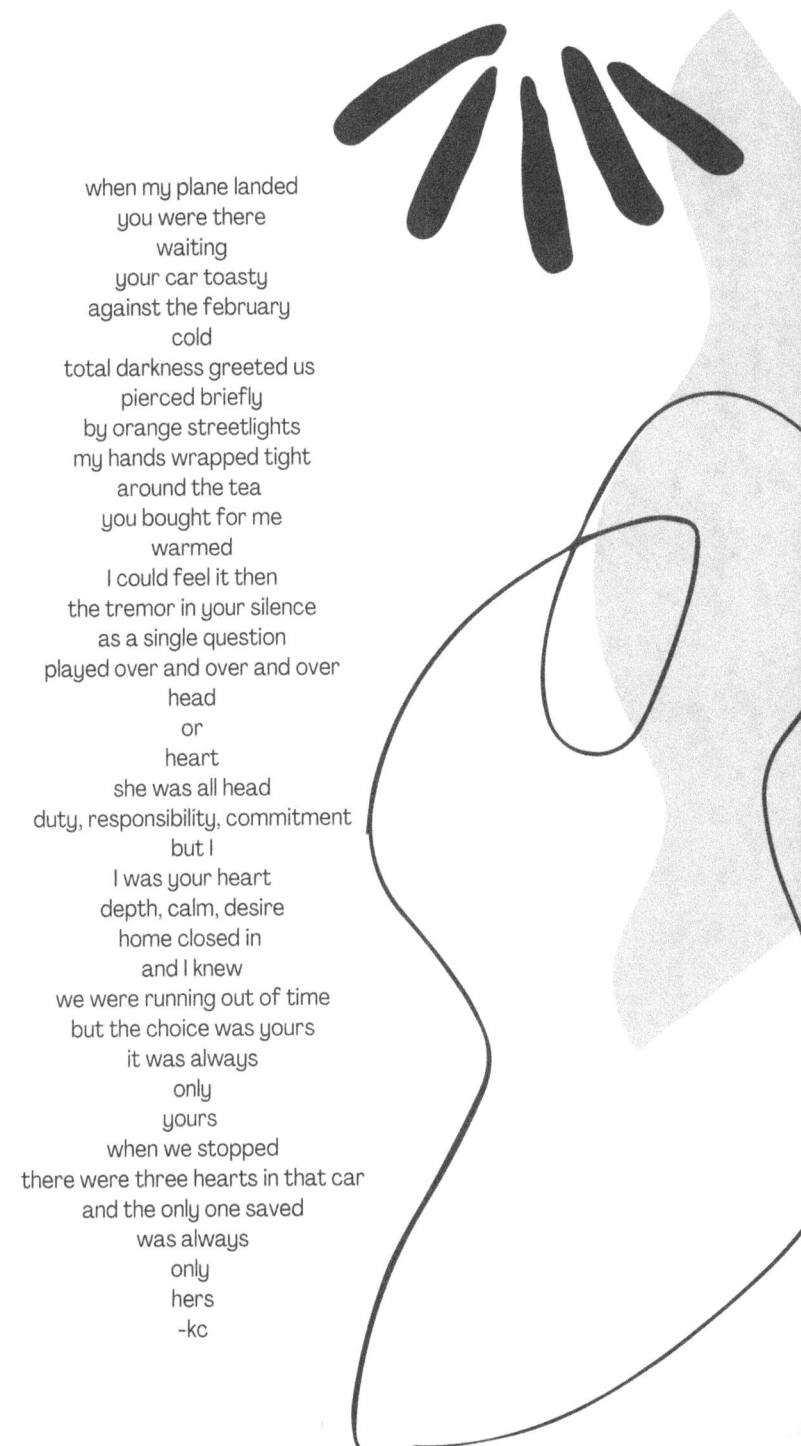

when my plane landed
you were there
waiting
your car toasty
against the february
cold
total darkness greeted us
pierced briefly
by orange streetlights
my hands wrapped tight
around the tea
you bought for me
warmed
I could feel it then
the tremor in your silence
as a single question
played over and over and over
head
or
heart
she was all head
duty, responsibility, commitment
but I
I was your heart
depth, calm, desire
home closed in
and I knew
we were running out of time
but the choice was yours
it was always
only
yours
when we stopped
there were three hearts in that car
and the only one saved
was always
only
hers
-kc

Ugly love

Remember when you called me crazy? Six months of flirting became six months of signals. That I interpreted, wrong.
Liar.
From the moment we met, we had this dance. It was in our eyes and our words and our bodies. It was in everything but the truth. You weren't single, though you wanted to be. We all knew it. You moved like your head lived in your pants and thought attention was something owed and not earned. It worked for awhile. The swagger on stage. The confidence in a crowd. You had a way of looking at me like you knew the sex would be great and that had a way of making me want it more. And I did. Want you.
More.
You told me it was all in my head then held my hand and kissed me. It made no sense. You made no sense.
I let you.
Our story ends there, though it's not much of a story. It's more like a footnote you find at the bottom of a page. A warning. If they lie to themselves, and they lie to their circle, they will, in fact, lie to you.
Don't believe them.
Or do.
Sometimes the sex really is that great.

you don't mean to
undress me
with your dad in the crowd
you do
your eyes
trace my collarbone
just a touch
below
my neck
hole in my jeans
hand in my pocket
six months
for
six minutes
in
six seconds
ruined
did she like
the way I tasted
when your lips parted?

ps
screw you
for leaving me
cold and discarded
-kc

Borrowed love

Remember that night in bed? I asked if you thought I was the one. You told me you didn't think, you knew. Your certainty was simple. It left me anxious. Not speechless, lost in the romance of it. Not full of love, though I suspect that existed beneath the layers I couldn't access yet.
Anxious.
How did you know? What did it look like? Feel like? Sound like? I had no answers; too ashamed to ask the questions. Out loud or inside. Because I knew, in the deepest parts of me, I wasn't. Beneath the layers. I knew you were wrong. It was the truest truth that existed between us. For us. We didn't get two. That wasn't how this worked.
And I was hers.
I was hers before I could ever be yours and I hated her for it. You saw us, and all we could be. I saw her, and all we should've been. You taught me how to see with my heart what the rest of me forgot. I'm sorry for that. You are the love I wanted before I understood the choice was never ours to make.
You are what could've been, would've been, if she hadn't been, first.

our eyes met
briefly
and I realized
she doesn't know
she doesn't
know
who I am
because if she did
her smile
wouldn't be kind
with her eyes
no
if she knew
who I was
her eyes
would've stilled
at the sight
the love
she thought
I reserved
no
it never lived
a moment
in my heart
-kc

Only love

It was late, after ten I think. We were talking about you. I can't remember how it started. Who brought you up. She didn't know your name, not until I said it. It came off my lips like a secret, so sacred I was afraid the air in that dingy bar would sully it. We huddled close, our knees knocking empty glasses. I told her about the day we met. Not the first date, with the dogs and the woods and the icy hills. The one before. With donuts and walks and nerves that ran wild.

I was so nervous, do you remember?

You offered to come see me, a meeting before we met. I changed my shirt four times. I don't know why; it was December, I wore a jacket. You only had a few minutes, so we walked.

45 passed.

You were running late. Can I hug you? The question stayed with me for hours. She looked at me then, the first pause in a story I couldn't stop telling. Our story. Her words came next. An observation so soft the world wouldn't hear it.

It wasn't anything I didn't already know.

behind my eyes
I saw it
a flash
making its way
through a single slit
in the curtains
lightning
I think
the kind that
awakens
so bright
and disappears
so fast
you wonder
was it ever really there
you were like that
I think
the lightning
so bright
yet gone
so fast
I often wonder
were you ever really
here
-kc

Hungry love

You weren't the best sex I've ever had. Still aren't.
You act like you are. I should hate that about you.
I don't.
When we see each other, it's clichéd. The room
stops. People disappear. And I swear, the world
would go up in flames if we let it.
Sometimes we do.
Afterwards, we seek each other out in the ashes.
We've been good lately. Faithful, some might call
it. You don't call. I don't text. Life has other plans.
Time passes and I almost forget. Almost. I think
it's over between us. The past is the past is the
past.
You call me.
It's over with that girl you swore that time meant
everything. Sometimes everything is just
something wrapped in thicker paper. We could do
better. I know there's someone out there who is
better.
We don't.
But it feels good, for a moment, to know we could.

it's only
at night
when I think about you
eyes closed
my skin hums
like you were already there
crawling beneath it
when you touch me
it happens again
the parts
I tried to love
go dark
my worth
wrapped around you
tied
with a ribbon
like a gift
you never asked for
a gift
I give you
still
-kc

High love

I took it personally, at first. When you didn't call. The first time, I waited by the phone. Not like they used to, with landlines glued to the wall in your kitchen.
Closer.
I carried you with me inside my pocket. Waiting. I tried to leave you behind. On the side table that houses my favourite book of poems. Inside the drawer of the desk I never seem to open. At a party with a friend whose name I can't remember.
It didn't last.
You felt safer in my pocket. I kept you there. You kept me there, too. Waiting. You never called. Not the first time I left. Or the fifth. Why did I keep going back to you? Why did you let me? We'll never know now, about any of it. I won't go back, you won't call.
But we'll wonder.

did you know
you were my last obstacle
to sobriety
the final fix
for me to kick

in protest
you became
the only habit
with a voice

but to my surprise
you were silent
the only one
who let me go
without so much
as a whisper
to come back
-kc

Lost love

It's not something I understand, what you're going through. I've never been in your shoes. There isn't a word I know or a feeling in my chest to show me what it's been like for you. I don't know what I'm asking of you. I just know I'm asking.
For a third chance.
To be yours and you mine, for good this time. Sound familiar?
I know. Maybe I'm full of shit.
Or maybe this time it's different. You and me, with all the glue and stickiness of a hard won love. You can't see inside my mind and heart and soul, but if you could you'd understand. For me, real love has always been a concept to aspire to, not a commitment to be made. It was always out of reach until you left and I finally tried not to.
It's for good.
I know it in the bones I'm made of and the heart I beat from. But I don't know what it's like to be you. I've never had to trust someone for a third time. And honestly, I can't imagine giving my heart to someone again, when they've given it back twice. I don't know if I could.
But I'm asking if you will.

it almost fell
the box
the only one
I keep
it moves with me
city to city
and
room to room
the small things
I carry
only pieces
of the big love
I let go
-kc

Paper love

When a new chapter begins, I clean. I get rid of things that no longer fit. It can be freeing, to declutter. I'm finished sorting old clothes, covered in dust, dealing with the final box in my closet. The one I keep because it's the only space I allow myself to hold on.
This box serves no purpose other than to reminisce, and remember. I forget, amidst the frayed sweaters and faded jeans, I put the realest part of you in there.
A handful of letters.
Or would you call them notes?
They were never mailed, left on our kitchen table for me to find when I got home. I should throw them out with the receipts from last spring.
I don't.
My dusty pants crease the duvet as I settle in, back in time, to words that caress my heart and cut it open at once.
It's not your words that hurt me; they're full of hope and love with a vulnerability that marks the pages. The pain comes from the memory of the girl who read them first. If she and I could trade places, I'd do it all differently.
There wouldn't be a box of letters I can't throw out but a home of things we keep together.

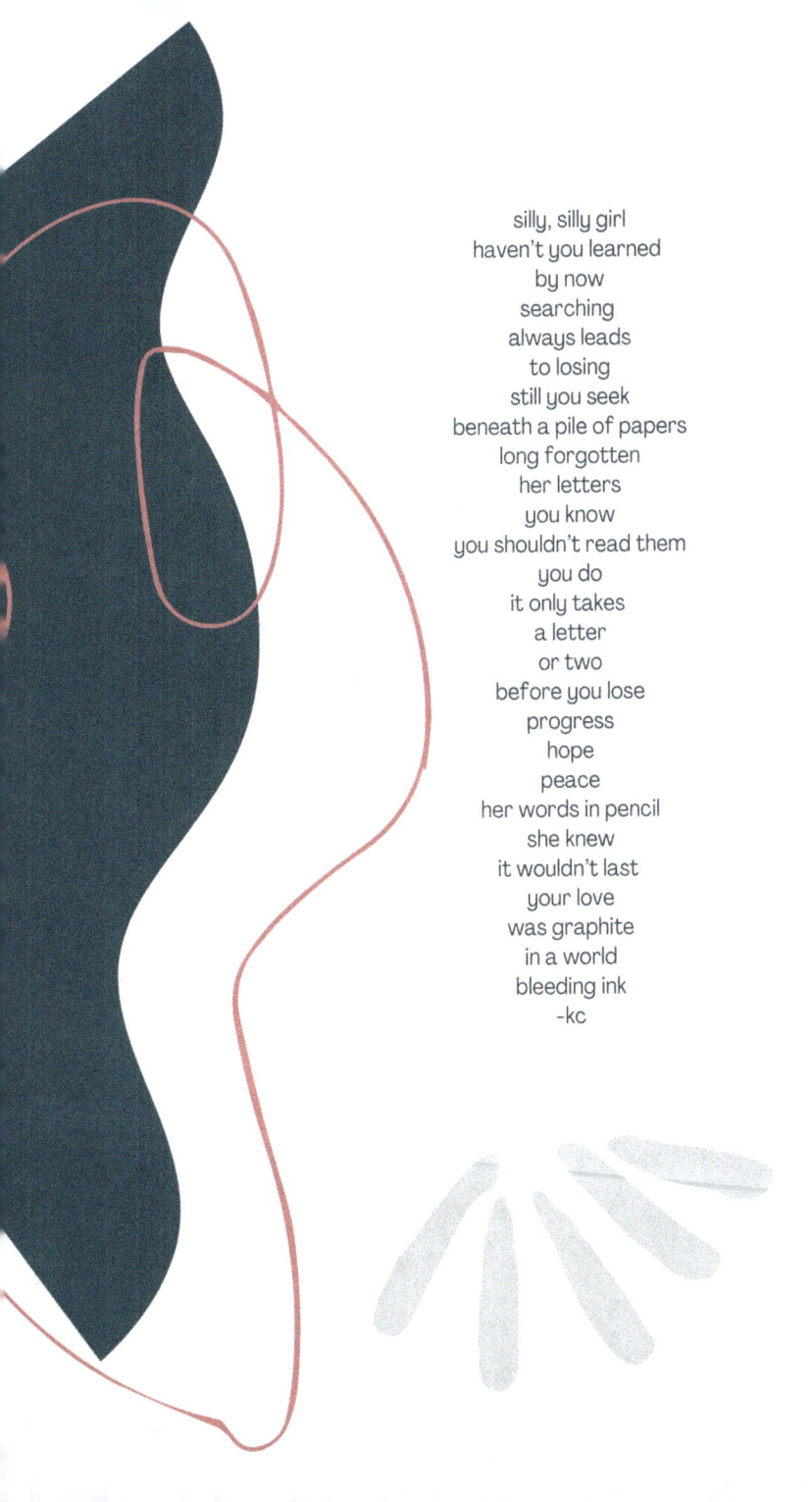

silly, silly girl
haven't you learned
by now
searching
always leads
to losing
still you seek
beneath a pile of papers
long forgotten
her letters
you know
you shouldn't read them
you do
it only takes
a letter
or two
before you lose
progress
hope
peace
her words in pencil
she knew
it wouldn't last
your love
was graphite
in a world
bleeding ink
-kc

Maybe love

There were so many nights I wanted to text you. I ran through possible messages in my head. Wished for birthdays and holidays to have an excuse. If I found the right combination of words, and sent it at the exact time, with the perfect excuse, everything would change.
Right?
I was willing to do anything to be with you. Whatever it took. I'd change jobs. Move cities. I would convince and reason and fight and beg and pray to whoever would listen if it meant getting you back. But I didn't.
Because what would I be getting?
Someone I needed to convince and reason and beg to be with me?
No, I'm not gonna fight for that anymore.
I want someone who knows. Someone who knows and feels it on their own and walks towards me. I'll meet halfway, but I'm not going the distance alone.
Not anymore.
Not even if I want to.

in an evening
it shifted
shoes on the welcome mat
do you know
the way a room bends
to greet you
imagine
my surprise
when you carried in
a rush of air
that left me
breathless
oh
what I wouldn't give
to know
intimately
the secret
your brown eyes
hold
to feel
intimately
the way
your soft lips
taste
if I had you
beneath my hands
for an evening
would it ruin me
with everyone
for a lifetime?
-kc

Wrong love

I could give you a million chances, and still, you would find a way to need a million and one. It doesn't stop. I never learn. I promise myself I will.
It's a lie.
You call and here I am, always. I tell myself that's love. Because it is. Isn't it? Without condition. For better and for worse.
You're both. And neither.
It doesn't occur to me, in all of this loving that I do for you, that it's supposed to go both ways. There isn't enough room to love us both, you show me. So we must choose. We always choose. It's you. It was never a choice. Demand falls off you like leaves in autumn. I scramble to catch them before they touch the ground. I can't. There's too many. There's always too many.
They fall.
I tell myself tomorrow will be different. Tomorrow never comes. You run out of lies. I run out of chances.
A million and one has finally become one too many.

loving you
hurt
and not in the way
pain
makes you strong
no

loving you
hurt
in the way
pain
makes you weak

the kind
that will force you
to your knees
not to
pray
for gratitude
but to
beg
for mercy
-kc

Quick love

The bumps and scars are old now. Grooves in my heart like roads filled with miles of moments that led me here. To you. Our knees touch, cross-legged and unprepared. Your necklace moves under my touch, gold beneath the black of your shirt. My fingers find it. To be closer to you, maybe.
Or to remind myself this is really happening.
I'm falling so fast for you the thought of it feels weightless. I imagine it's how skydivers feel when they're about to jump. The anticipation. The knowledge of what's to come.
But also, the uncertainty.
No matter how much you think about it, nothing can prepare you for when it actually happens. The risk is without description. It simply must be felt. I think the same is true about love. I'm standing on the edge of the plane now. The door is open, a sound so loud my head gives way to my heart. The next step will be the hardest and easiest thing I have ever done.
It's no longer a choice of if, but a question of when.

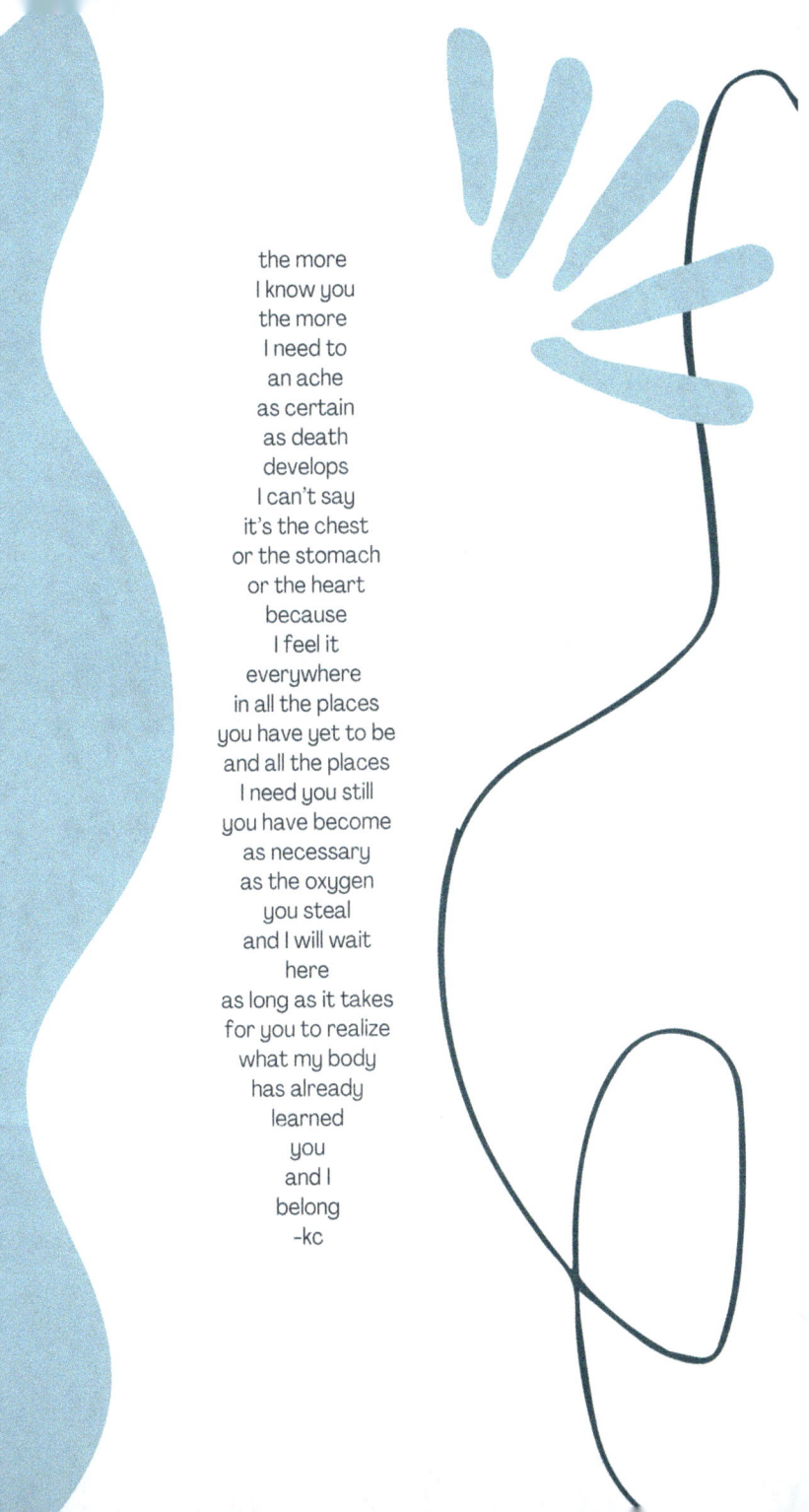

the more
I know you
the more
I need to
an ache
as certain
as death
develops
I can't say
it's the chest
or the stomach
or the heart
because
I feel it
everywhere
in all the places
you have yet to be
and all the places
I need you still
you have become
as necessary
as the oxygen
you steal
and I will wait
here
as long as it takes
for you to realize
what my body
has already
learned
you
and I
belong
-kc

Jealous love

We're not the type of people who fall in love easily. You say it with a certainty I can't quite match. I try. Eyes locked and pinky promised. It wasn't a statement you wanted to stand in alone. A plea forms in your eyes without reaching your lips. I know what you want, can see it in the curve of your smile and the furrow of your brow. Cards sit between us, your hands fumbling with the deck. You make eye contact sparingly, burdened by the desire you find there. I'm trying to think of when I knew I lost you.

Was it against the pillows, spine rigid like the set of your mouth?

Maybe it was on your knees, head bent in overwhelm.

I lied to you that night. It didn't matter.

You already knew.

What would it be like, I asked, to have a love like theirs?

It wasn't subtle. My heart hinged on the answer.

Brave.

I wouldn't know, you replied.

Final.

what I wanted
was simple
a trade
between friends
your love
for mine
with a promise
to feel
for once
what it's like
to have someone
love you
and show it

where would I be
lately
if I had a love
that met me
on the outside
instead
of a hunger
that kept me
on the inside

her mood
no longer
moving
like the rise
and fall
of the tide
but steady
like the sweet
rhythm
of rain
-kc

Ordinary love

When did I realize?
She wanted it to be easy. Something to search for in every person that came after.
My answer?
Coming home to you.
It was August. The kind of heat that mattes your hair to your neck and runs droplets down your spine. I went out after work. The job was new and friends were scarce. I stayed out well past bedtime, exchanging our nine thirty for midnight. The highway was empty on the drive home, a Tuesday unlikely to draw traffic this late. Moving through the house on tippy toes, my eyes meet the dark, familiarity in the shadows. Teeth brushed and pjs on I slip into bed, careful. You lay on your side, facing away from me. Watching you in silhouette my eyes adjust to the rest. I see you clearly in that darkness. Even though it's late, and you're fast asleep, and it's selfish, I curl up around you. My cold skin thaws around a warmth only you can give me. Arm around your waist, I bury my face in your neck, breathing in until your scent fills my lungs. Every breath that is mine, becomes oxygen that is ours.
Until we are one, once again.
I didn't know home as a feeling, before you. I never understood the sense of arrived that comes from being in a place that houses and holds and heals you.
Now I do.

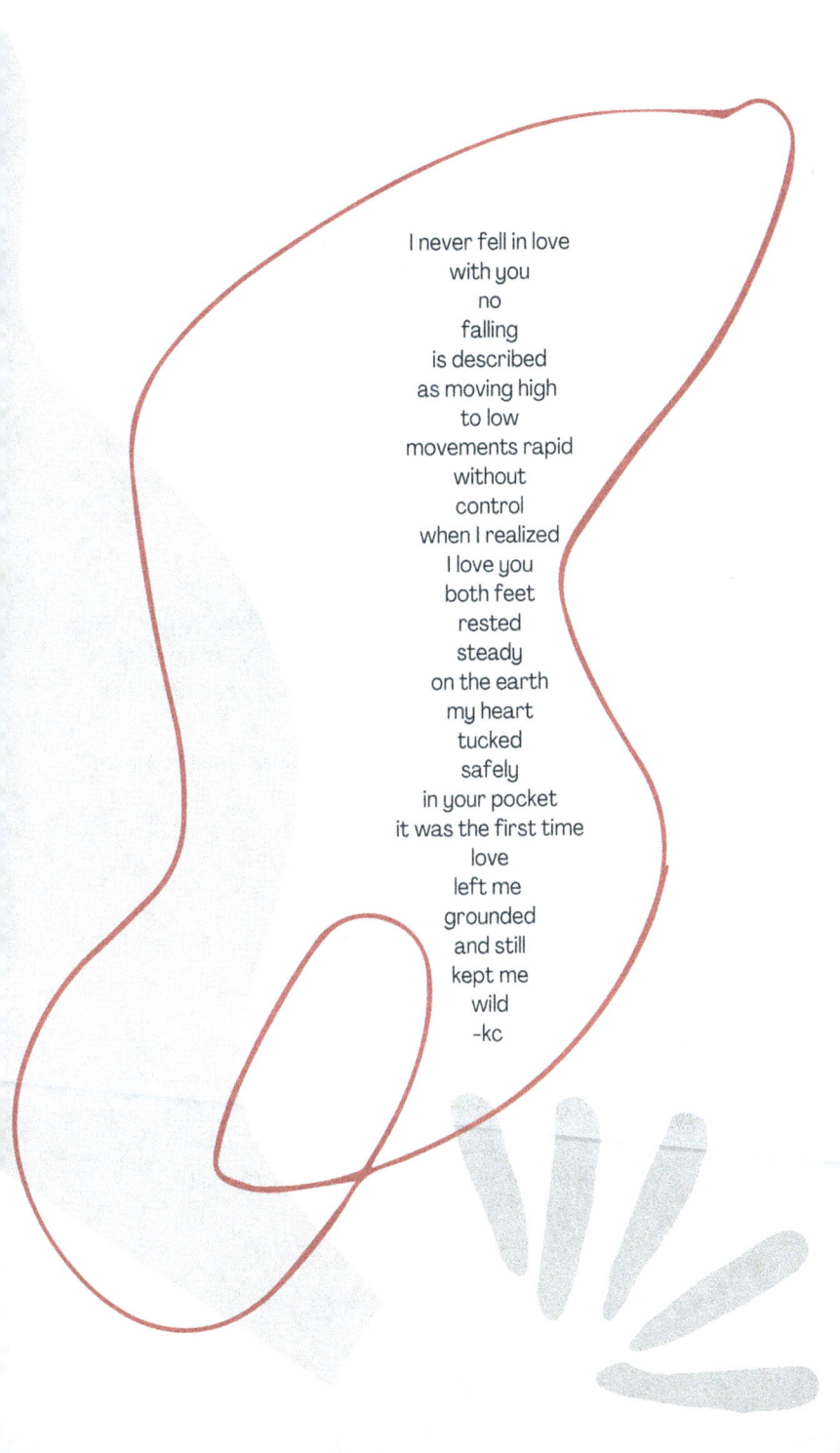

I never fell in love
with you
no
falling
is described
as moving high
to low
movements rapid
without
control
when I realized
I love you
both feet
rested
steady
on the earth
my heart
tucked
safely
in your pocket
it was the first time
love
left me
grounded
and still
kept me
wild
-kc

Steady love

I was always running. When I was young, I ran from responsibility. Punishment. Parents. As I got older, the running got farther. Faster. Trickier. I was no longer avoiding a messy bed, or messy consequences, or messy conversations.

It was relationships. Apartments. Cities.

I moved from person to person and place to place, bags packed, never staying long enough to need what's in them. The running wasn't always bad. I ran towards an opportunity I was excited about, a person I was in love with, a city I'd only dreamed of. Sometimes it was good.

Mostly, it wasn't.

From the beginning, I convinced myself if you couldn't face a problem, you could outrun it. Turns out, you can run, but problems will follow. They always follow. Every relationship. Apartment. City.

No bag left behind.

Eventually, they became too heavy to carry. I needed to put them down, and let things go. I needed to find people to help me carry them. I did both. Running is no longer an answer, but a pastime.

Staying is no longer a chore, but a gift.

at thirteen
I'd traveled
by window
often

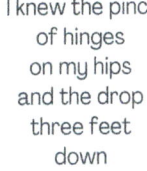

I knew the pinch
of hinges
on my hips
and the drop
three feet
down

and every time
I landed
on my feet
freedom
tasted sweet
on my tongue
yet

after so many
years
of jumping
and running
and leaving
walking out
on you
felt like

the first time
I've ever
left home
-kc

Someday love

Why are you here?
The question becomes the first and only that day. I don't answer, taking in the room. There are four painted walls. A few photos. Some books on the shelf. Four chairs. Chips of nail polish fall in my lap as silence fills the space. I could deflect. Ask you a question instead. Make a joke. Tell you I don't know, a customary response for me. I hesitate not because I don't know what to say, but because I don't know how.

Do I tell her about your smile, and the way it leads moment for moment?

Should I start with your goodbye kiss, eyes closed and heart open, or your hello dance, love always the loudest thing in the room?

She's asking a single question, but what she doesn't realize is you're made up of a million answers. To explain you would be like trying to describe a sunset to someone who's never seen it. Words fail.

Of course, we're not here because I've witnessed the beauty of a sunset. No. We're here because I held it in my hands, with all the beauty that it is, and walked away from it.

I'm here because I loved you and I left you and I need someone to tell me why.

why
why
why
did it take me so long
to see
you were nothing
but tendrils
of smoke
clouding my eyes
burning my lungs
curling my skin
I shed
every layer
until I was nothing
but the heart
that beats
beneath
stained skin
and the bones
that settle
underneath
deep yearning
-kc

Hopeful love

How do you know you love her? I turn the question over in my mind so many times it feels upside down. I asked myself this question in every relationship I've had since they started.
How is this one different?
I looked for the answer in pages of books and posts online and notes from experts and friends whose love I thought I wanted. I looked everywhere for a truth that was never further than under my rib cage.
I love you. I know I love you. I've loved you since the first time I saw you. A saviour with a shovel in a winter storm. Everything was black, from your coat to your car to the night in your eyes. You saved me that night. But not for the reason you remember.
You loved me so much, so well, I believed you.
I let you.
I love you.
I know I love you because I don't think about it. I've never had to.

I love you. And I left you.
You were my ultimate sacrifice; to give up something you can't live without, for someone you love more than yourself. That's what I did. I let us go to save you from who I'd become. I know it didn't make sense then. I hope you can see it now.
Because we are inevitable.
If I don't have you in this lifetime, I'm not worried.
I know I'll find you in the next.
We're fated that way.

Love
will disappoint you
Love
will leave you
Love
will shatter you

but
if you let it in

Love
will surprise you
Love
will carry you
Love
will heal you

for all the pain
it causes
and all the questions
it asks

Love
is the only thing
in life
worth fighting for.
-kc

thank you
for reading
and thank you
for supporting a queer artist
with something to say
who was terrified to share it with the world
but is doing it anyway
you fulfilled my dream today
if there's one thing I can do for you in return
let it be to inspire you to follow one of your own
-kc

for more of my writing check out dearqueerpoet.com

www.ingramcontent.com/pod-product-compliance
Lightning Source LLC
Chambersburg PA
CBHW071317080526
44587CB00018B/3262